Teaching a Wild Thing

Teaching a Wild Thing

Poems by

Kindra McDonald

Cover design by Shay Culligan
Cover art designed by Adam Greene

ISBN: 978-1-63980-214-2

Kelsay Books
502 South 1040 East, A-119
American Fork, Utah 84003
Kelsaybooks.com

For my sisters, all of you, the in-laws, the outlaws, the sisters in
words, I love you.
And this always, because of Adam, thank you for chipping away
my shell, for giving me the wild.

*When the sun goes down/and the dreams grow teeth and the beasts
come out and cast their long shadows/Every time they start, I'll be
right here with you, I'm not afraid of the dark.*
—Josh Ritter

Acknowledgments

Thank you to the editors of the journals in which the following work has previously appeared:

300 Days of Sun: "Long Distance"
Artemis Journal: "Things that have died this month"
Autumn Sky Poetry Daily: "Lessons: December 2020"
Cathexis Review Northwest: "Folding"
Cupola: "What I am trying to say . . ."
Drunk Monkeys: "Colloquial"
Green Ink Press: "Vision"
Harbor Review: "Waiting"
Haunted Waters Press: "Absence," "A cure for blue"
Headline Poetry and Press: "Could We Live?"
Moonstone Arts Love & the Pandemic: "Perfection, still"
Pine Hills Review: "Origins"
Plants and Poetry Press: "All the animals I met this summer . . ."
Stirring Literary Magazine: "Callinectes Sapidus"
SWWIM: "Almost Free"
TAB the Journal of Poetry and Poetics: "Humbled," "Imagine"
Tiny Seed Journal: "Newborn"
Wild Roof Journal: "Tropical Depression"

Thank you, reader, for holding this book in your hands. For supporting your local poets and small presses.

Contents

Imagine

I was a key
an attic token
a hanging ribbon
castoffs slumped
with ancient dolls
I was holy thighs
a strawberry swelling
mint leaves floating
in peach tea
a May chestnut
I spun pinballs wild
a flicker of fairies
revealed in flame
I found myself split
a box in another box
in a U-Haul
there's a reason
we scatter like salt
every time I want to burn
away, I remember
I was taught to save things.

Origins

1.

At the whaling museum in Newport: wandering through rooms of scrimshaw, carved bones of whales, teeth and tusk, ribs and cartilage illuminated by soft exhibit light. Glowing mermaids, billowing sails and lost fishermen, so many versions of the female form. Memory carved in solitude. I learn *wale* is the plank alongside a wooden ship that protects the hull from damage, it is also the ridge of fabric on my corduroy pants, the swooshing sound of my legs rubbing together.

2.

I teach my students in Beijing about mammals and birds: they are both warm-blooded, though birds lay eggs and mammals have live births. We work again and again on *whale,* how it is a mammal, not cold-blooded like fish that also live in the sea. They pronounce it *"well"* and we've just learned that a well is where you get water; when I say *well done,* both thumbs enthusiastically up, that is a different kind of well.

3.

The summer we all watched the one whale: how she carried her dead calf on her back for 17 days and more than 1,000 miles in a tour of grief while we all looked on in wonder, a solidarity of loss. After this year of thrashing, it is confirmed this whale is pregnant again. Researchers have tracked her pod by satellite. This seems a miracle. Every time I see our planet from space it makes me believe in a reverse Pangea, that the continents might slowly move toward each other the way a cello leans on the shoulder of a musician.

4.

In the church basements of my childhood: every funeral farewell lunch featured shining Jell-O salads. They glistened like stained glass, fruit suspended in molds of rings and braids, all jiggling companionably next to a jellied tuna salad in the shape of a whale.

5.

My students watch me cry on our video screen. *Whale,* I say. Well done. Wail.

6.

I have spent a year of days slowly teaching a wild thing to eat from my hand, only to find it dead, matted fur, broken paw. I wail to the ground, to the clouds, to the sea. Well. Well. How wail is a high-pitched cry of pain—it's what we do when we are mourning, a parade of grief we wake to each morning. We hold a wake for the dead, this language is impossible.

This is how I ask for help

My showers last so long
my teeth chatter from the running
cold that's turned me numb
my fingers blue and foreign.
I take to washing dishes carelessly
dropping plates and shattering glasses
shards I scoop up, hold on to a little long
tuck in a pocket or wear like a charm.
I remember to shower only when
I catch a glimpse of my hair
a slick drip across my forehead
all of it too long and uncombed.
My ribs are two sides of a stripped zipper
rows of metal teeth, a hook and a hollow
the best of me and the beast of me crack
open between my breasts and animal heart.
I can't sleep
is all I do, I can't
sleep is all, I can't sleep
is all I do.

My thoughts spin away like my missing organs—
ovaries and appendix, gallbladder and spleen
speak to me in riddles, betray me one by one.
I feel the word on the tip of my tongue
a tongue twister kind of word, like the winning word
of a spelling bee lodged in the roof of my mouth
stung tongue swollen in my mouth, I feel it like braille
with the whorls of my fingerprints pulled from skin
this word feel it on my tongue, I'm not hungry
but my mouth is lonely for this word, and this is how
I ask for help.

Long-distance

I call my sister and get the number
for the Suicide Prevention Hotline
because after raising her children
and sending them into their own lives

she returned to school to certify a lifelong
talent of strong ears and listening shoulders
a career that has called her like neon arrows
pointing cracked hearts and broken people

to her, while I never tell the many times
I have needed the help she offers now
in her room she has carefully curated—
made welcome with oversized chairs

sharpened crayons and weighted blankets
I call her nearly daily to hear her voicemail
which says *if this is an emergency
call 911 or the Suicide Prevention Hotline*

which I listen to again as she takes on
the weight of others until her frame
is birdlike and cushioned only with stories
of sorrow, I will not tell her

my own. I call my sister, I call
my sister, I call and recite the number
for the Suicide Prevention Hotline
her voice soft and reassuring

I hang up.

Apricity

Is the term for the warmth of sun in winter
and this is a gift for bees and flowers
a reminder that God wastes nothing
in our lives even every little misery.
We don't lean into those we don't trust
and frame by frame she works
unloading the heavy burdens of winter's
work, the stores of food from honeybees
each cell in each frame protected by wax
and apricity is so close to apiary
this collection of beehives reminds me
it is so close to aviary and did you know
if you keep a bird in a circular cage
it will go mad? With no place to hide
her face in a crook of an endless
spinning circle with no angles
searching for a corner to retreat
to, and every fighter needs a corner
every winter—warmth.

Waiting

In the complete women's care office
babies line the walls in gilded picture frames
the siblings in the field at golden hour
backlit by the sun, awash in something
that must be halo-light, and the portrait
of the triplets, all captured in various stages
of movement, I breathe and see their eyes blink
their mouths move, and all the infants
swaddled in pink and blue, one newborn
splayed in a giant scallop shell, raw and quivering
they call my name, take me to a room without
children on the wall, just gulls lifting into the sky
one by one.

Flawed

I've become an   empty   rental house
my brain   an oval gasp   open ditch

I mean changing like an apology
or a favor, only a sliver (   ) of character left.

                    My skin a costume or animal's pelt
a naked flame I glance at lethal   like a razor

shocking every time I can identify myself
the wife, the mother, I could have   been.

Due

There was a spring baby boom
in the office where I worked.
Don't drink the water, they joked
as all around me the pregnant women grew
each day and the cubicle walls
pressed in.

Shower after shower all pink
and blue so frosting sweet
and all the guesses and wives' tales
carrying high and craving salt
daily updates like weather reports
the constant rotating due-date lotto.
I would shrink in my desk each morning
sick with worry, while all of them leaned
in and spun a sewing needle up and down
we are pink-cheeked giddy for girls
side to side, we toast and clap for boys.

Swelling month after month in secret.

At home I watch the squirrels steal
stuffing from my swing cushions
building nests in the tree. The thrush
is busy all morning swiping moss
and pine straw, my knotted hair
and strewn tissues make a home.
Butterflies rest fast on goldenrod
and aster, the ones with eyes
are God's spies. The dragonflies
dance and dip, a devil's darning needle
left to its own device will sew your mouth shut.
It's my turn to make the weekly
cake and the egg I crack has two yolks
glossy eyes wobble and I wonder this time

how to divine this break, it is either twins
or death. One in every thousand hens
lay double eggs, one in every thousand
babies are born with teeth.

The mothers tell me my cakes are the sweetest.

Small Fists

Days of adored
lullabies like
fruit without seeds
roses made of ribbons
of course lurking
the lightning of shame
accept I'm afraid
in the heart—wilted
I was hurting, waiting
for truth like a hummingbird
fluttering endlessly

Refills

The nurse looks at my chart
both parents are dead, yes
that is why I am here.
I forget how to smile and sometimes to speak.
She hands me tissues and leaves.
This is just the way you're wired,
the doctor says, *use the refills.*

Prescriptions damp in my hands
I walk to a park, find the space between
ladybugs and petals. In a long line
of cherry blossom trees, gaudy in bloom
showy twirling dresses of falling pollen
I kneel, press my palms to the moss
carpet warm from sun. On my stomach
cheek to the earth, feeling
for an answer somewhere
between bare branch
and bud bloom.

On the ground I smell lilacs. The tree roots
from this angle are a fallen constellation
it took me so long to find a place
that smells like home, maybe someday
I'll forget that their zodiac sign was Cancer.

Could We Live?

This spring all the grocery stores have run
out of yeast. We are searching the aisles
for this single-cell organism, begging
our neighbors for flour, trying to track
down sourdough starters. We have all
been baking bread and I break bread
virtually over computer communion
with the stale saltine I found in the cabinet
and dip into some cooking sherry, the sacrilege
of this sacred act.
We have all been baking bread
it changes the smell of worry
in our homes to comfort. The melting
butter is like a pool of sun, filling
our stomachs with something
like love, but mostly when we knead
the dough, warm and living, soft
and pliant, it feels like hugging,
it feels like human touch.
If we could live on bread

alone; we could live on
bread that would somehow
make us whole, together alone.

Death of a Ghost

Dear K,

Could we send letters back in time?
Crying now over the death of a ghost

a weight so buoyant the pallbearers
could be mice, mournful and misty-eyed.
No harm has come to pass,
I might say. Wishful thinking,

you would say. Hindsight is 20/20—
and we'd both laugh. If I wrote a letter

to myself, I'd hold it up to the light
warm the invisible ink over fire
watch the alphabet spiral to the clouds
like smoke, hear the sad, same three notes

of a bugle leading a funeral procession.
You could turn my letters into words

or into paper airplanes you could race
or crash or hatch into new life, you would say
I told you so.

Love, K

Wish

What I want is the moon
hung from the bend
in the cliff
shedding light
like small stones
beneath my palms
an afterthought
of crescents
on my skin.

What I want is to quit
a shadow I can shake off
and slink away cowardly
chasing a lunar eclipse
soundtracks of black and white westerns
playing wherever I hide.
What I want is to lean into the steeple
of dawn like an afterthought
with a loose-fitting shirt
and soft soil on my knees
the moon hung
from the bend in the cliff.

Absence

When I tuck the son I don't have into his bed at night
I find acorns and pinecones in his sheets, little bits of day
he has carried with him into dreams and I'll collect them on a shelf
and label them as artifacts, evidence of loss.
The daughter I don't have has spent hours searching
for shark's teeth on the beach, her wet hair sticking
to her cheek, she'll shed sand from her skin that I'll
catch in a jam jar put in the cabinet to glisten in the dark.

For weeks I have heard heavy equipment groaning
at the edge of the neighborhood, coming from the pool
that for the past few summers has become quiet, emptied
of cookouts and swim lessons, birthday parties and sunbathers.
The same pool my husband swam in as a child when our house
was his grandparent's home and he'd spend summers lazing
feet dangling in the deep end, popsicle sticky in his hand. On my
daily walks I have taken to detouring past the pool, see it is closing

For good, a community vote to make it disappear. The lifeguard seat,
pool house and playground dismantled, swing by swing. The rusty
fence, old eyesore, ripped out in pieces, a puzzle back in a box. Each
day's progress is a grave in reverse. The pool filled in with dirt.

Somewhere in our backyard, my love buried a bird. When he was
ten it crashed into the sunroom windows. Three days later he dug it
up to see if it had rose again. Imagine his confusion over
resurrection. I told him I buried Barbie heads under a tree in my
yard, hoping to sprout new dolls that looked like me. I don't say I
imagine what our children look like.

I have given up on sleep and slip out at night. I step easily over caution tape and walk towards what would have been the edge of the deep end, all is soft and level. Was there ever a hole in this ground? Pretend my feet are dangling cool and swinging in the water, the jump, the splash—

I lay pressed on the newly turned soil, my face even with grass seedlings pushing to life, and I don't know if I'm floating or drowning—these days, it's hard to tell.

An Idiom in Six Letters

You know what blood looks like in a black and white video?
—John Prine

Afraid of one's own (   ), cast a long (   ), become a
(   ) of your former self, old sins have long (   ), valley of
the (   ) of death, beyond a (   ) of a doubt, five o'clock
(   ), under someone's (   ), a false friend and a (   )
stay only while the sun shines, take the (   ) for the substance,
wear yourself to a (   ), wrangle for an ass's (   ), coming
events cast their (   ) before them, valley of the (   ) of
death.

In the Six Days Without Power After Hurricane Isabel, We Try to Save Our Marriage

Category 1 winds: 74–95 mph—very dangerous

We have left our rolling hills and basements for this new town of flooding and bridge lifts and Weather Channel Acts of God, as if a change of scenery could change us, but wherever you go, there you are. In the days of build-up and tension you stock supplies and horde water, there is lots of alcohol. I want to leave, you want to stay, and so we play at tug of war and you are always stronger. We lose power before the winds even start. The late summer heat settles in, the quiet pours over us like concrete.

Category 2 winds: 96–110—extremely dangerous

By noon the howling has taken on a musical quality, whistling and punctuating our yelling with its rising pitch and crescendo of ripping shingles. You climb onto our porch rail to repair the flapping siding, I grip you by your belt loops hold you steady, wishing we never moved here, never married, wish we never met, you spit as the wind whips the house, shutters fly like magic carpets, what is left to hold on to?

Category 3 winds: 111–129—devastating damage

Debris is flying and falling, we retreat to our corners then square off again as dusk settles in and we are gray shadows slipping past each other. We do what we do when we've lost our voices, toss our bodies toward each other wave after wave, drag sheets from room to room, re-enact a camping trip over candlelight and tin beans, tell soft stories that make us smile. The eye is over us, quiet and calm and even in this dark we see that white-knuckled love is not enough.

Category 4 winds: 130–156—catastrophic damage

Days without power, milk curdling sour, the rotting drip of thawing meat and humidity hangs heavy as a vow. We are wrung out from crying, sick and sleepless. Our lives swim through the flooded kitchen, a floating champagne flute, a sterling cake server. Windows shatter and 12 packs come and go in fever dreams of broken bottles and picture frames. The pines are ripped from the lawn and it's obvious how shallow the roots are.

Category 5 winds: 157 mph or higher—recovery may take months to years

The neighbor says it will be weeks before the road is clear. It's prison, and we beg each other for parole. We dry out, pack our hearts in separate boxes, mitigate the hemorrhage in the roof. Without streetlights and screen glare we can see the stars so clearly, funny how we know they're always there. When the generators around us roar to life, there is nothing left to say.

I Do(e)

The Dressing Room (south) welcomes our brides: Trilby,
Carly, Angie, Cher, arrows pierce chalkboard hearts—
the shop's logo a rack of antlers, warning
betrothed that soon their veils will turn and bristle
twisted crown of points, velvet fur rubbed empty
after the rut, the hunt, disembodied fawn.
Remember how to field dress a deer? Skinned, stripped
humped to truck, gun rack full, mounted on the wall
hard-won prize, fur dew-damp, taken at dawn, dream

they'll wake as hunters, smell blood on sheets, aim vows
frozen in headlights pointing the dark way home.

How are you?

Is close to *are you over it?*

Depression doesn't care
it isn't angry
or brave
just *lies* hidden in the word *smile*
stunts unable to be acted out
a stream of chemicals
that appear to be important
it's a quieter softer subdued
negative of my portrait
a puzzle on a knife blade
the long pause on a cliff
a stream of ships pretty
but sinking

somewhere is a sweet bird
of hope I believe I can locate

What I am trying to say is my brain is full of honeybees

The honeybee has officially been considered the most important living creature on earth and it will be so until it is no longer here.

That they are buzzing and thrumming
that they are fanning the temperature
of this apiary in my head so I am always
92 degrees—most crime is seasonal.
It started when I gargled, brushed my teeth
and buzzed, I spoke in hums and soon
wings caught in my lungs, fluttering.
I am asking you, please to blow smoke
in my ear, to know the difference
between a wasp and its fuzzy cousin.
I am hurting. Sometimes my skin becomes
so touch tender and swollen even pollen dust
burns when it settles like light on my chin.
It will be a winter full of honey synapses
I will melt like sugar in your mouth
the more I think the louder the buzz.
My hands are the size of fig leaves.
Have you tried to grasp a flower, stroke
a cheek, when your hands are as big as fig
leaves? Clumsy. The medulla is so syrupy
thick my heart becomes clogged, my arteries
carry atrocities away, my veins ferry pain
that is 80% sugar, but still not sweet.

How it seems more possible than ever
to disappear. In every picture ever taken
of me my eyes are closed. Now you can catch me
lifting up, hovering, just about to take flight. What
I am trying to say is, listen.

Les Méres Extraordinaires

I believe all mothers
grow eyes in the back
of their head, somewhere
between the third trimester
and birth, the sclera form
then pupils and iris
and upon the severing
of an umbilical cord
the dome of the cornea
focusing light and love
sharp and clear
so that wherever
her children are
she can see them
when she bows
her head to pray
blinks or dreams
of extraordinary
calamities only she
can prevent.

Feel a little sad

But do not flinch
if you feel the target
of decades of practice
in this game show life
heavy on your back.
In this world of wish and blush
words are a strong right arm
death is a pearl harvested
and swallowed hard.
This life-size cutout of me
is the absence of a trigger,
the presence of a fighter.
I do not flinch.

Folding

Whenever a recipe says to fold an ingredient
I think of origami and the slow and deliberate
folding of paper, corner to corner, the creasing
that makes wings, or beaks, or clever tufts
of feathers that can fan. A therapist once

showed me how a crane could be a wish.
I often do things I know will hurt me
like eating dough raw, eggs barely
blended into flour, as if salmonella's
stomach cramps would be welcome
respite from this numbness. Sometimes
when I'm slicing tomatoes, I think of how the knife
would feel on my wrist, how breaking the skin would
be as satisfying as the snap of a string bean

the cut of the cucumber into perfect cold slices
and it's hard to change that thought. Now, though
I'm folding egg whites into batter for angel food
cake. A cake that I have eaten, (somehow without
tasting), after every funeral I have ever been to

and because we can't have funerals right now, I am
making this cake that I know will hurt me. My stomach
growls as the angel food rises. I'm startled to find I feel—
I do know how.

Lost

Lately I have found myself
so deep in thought, I have lost
minutes of time unaccounted for
like tonight as I was slicing
tomatoes for dinner, cutting
sweet corn off in neat rows
and arranging basil on a plate
like little festive flags.
I thought about how vibrant
summer food is, how it takes
so little effort to make it look
like I have tried to nourish someone
instead of simply making do
with what I have.

Yesterday I lost the better part
of an hour massaging kale
for dinner, I had read it makes
it easier to digest and life has seemed
so hard to swallow it is a small chore
to make our salad more tender. Somewhere
in that lost time I forgot about my mom
masked and alone boarding a plane
where she promises she won't be arm
to breast, cheek to shoulder
with the travelers around her
glowing feverishly close.

Think of Such Things

Phil 4:8

Now trapped inside these four walls
lonely racing raindrops down glass panes
hands pressed to a past
my memory fogs like breath

Now when the home movies
of my life reel behind me
in Super 8 pastels of pink and blue
shadows dancing remember
how well the bathtub holds me
how the chair knows my shape
but can't contain me, when
I was water I curled and crashed
shocking cold and wild how I always
returned to the place I was born

When I was a tree I shook light
like golden tinsel, held up the shade,
drank in the rain, lifted the climbers
and each season shed and bloomed
grew again towards sky

When I was a bird I was a guide
to the fisherman, pointing out each
speckled scale, I knew rain was coming
by how my feathers tingled, when my
wings tired no matter how far I was
I knew just how to find home, building
nests from the bones of fish

The best of me mourns the salt spray
on my face, how my hair made a cape
behind me in the breeze, how the spider
climbs the spout not fearing rain

We are mirror selves, my best and me
when I was a child my heartbeat
was violins, my bare feet slapped
the gritty wood boardwalk immune
to splinters, skipping through surf
and spinning sand of praise and song

Open the door, put one foot in front
learn to run again even knowing I'll end
where sky meets sea—
this is faith to leap
becoming again and again and again

Almost Free

Heaven
is the moon swinging
hand under hand
just to hug the ground
with light strong as knots
Bright egg
dance gingerly
dance delirious
a swan drowned
a half thigh
a lemon pout
moon a lit firefly hum
in my ear

Broken Ghazal for the Burning World

Every summer California burns, this year the whole west coast is blazing, come rain, claim us. Winds carry smoke east and my window patch of sky is hazy blame. Who will claim us?

I'd like to think that my first word was *word,* but it can't be overheard, those gone rotted brains who taught me, we're all born, we're not all raised. Add to the list of things we love that hurt us.

Here is a spell to overcome despair: one full moon, a peeled apple, two overlapping coffee stains all the dog-eared corners of your favorite book, this fallen leaf, this breath, inhale, now train us.

I want a funeral procession so long the blinking lights of cars stretch from Granby Street to Main these thoughts are little embers, little sparks, a light as lonely as a corner payphone, change us.

Today I disappeared. For how long, I do not know. I walked until I vanished, call me insane. The cat brings in secrets on her fur, I've only bug bites as proof I'm here at all, this pain, just us.

Justice never comes and fury grows with each delay, excuses bubble like shook champagne pinky promise me we are more than links in a broken chain, what will it take to sustain us?

Life is not less than property, if property is greater than life if all the sand were counted grains and all the grains could fill the stomach of a sparrow, what is the hour when we can explain us?

If this house was saved by prayer, but every smoldering home around is rubble, who gains the ear of God, who holds the sparrow, God prunes us so that we may bear fruit, bless us.

Oh, the things I would burn to create the perfect smokey eye, the seething of our ruin, vain in my mirror of truth. Why was I told if a boy is mean, he liked me? Our shadows remain us.

Let's greet the day in peace, make breakfast for the moths, wish for the soaking of a kind rain, let's feast on this flower, sweep ash into silver campaigns for our future. Who now will claim us?

Callinectes Sapidus

At the mouth of the Chesapeake Bay
the sun sets slow and gilded
turning the fair-haired heads
bobbing on the shore into
glowing halos
I am teaching families the art
of crabbing, a catch
and release program.

With a serrated knife in a bucket
I have cut chicken into chunks
laid them raw on the sand
to be speared and thrown out on cast lines
I had spent hours untangling
while listening to the news reports
of another mass shooting.

This one is home, here. Did you know
you can feel a soft crab's heartbeat
just by holding them carefully? I am no longer
bothered by the rough handling of the chicken.
Skin pools like gelatin, the seagulls circle
above this buffet as I describe how blue crabs
shed their shells more than 20 times in their life.

How to identify the males from the females—
the rounded apron of the Sook, the triangular
point of the Sally, the narrow, sharp spear
of the Jimmy, (what we order for parties
every summer), unfolding the newspapers
not reading headlines
cracking and breaking the shells, the cobalt
shot across their front claws—
their Latin name *means beautiful, savory*
swimmers and as the families lure the crabs

to shore skittering sideways into my waiting
net we hoist a female, hugely pregnant, a sponge
caviar black, throbbing on her belly. As the children
swarm around, her pincers click out codes
of warning. When the eggs are first formed
they are bright orange, then shift to dark brown
then deep black, this, I pause is the development

of millions of individual baby crab eyes

all of them watching, being watched
as I lower the net in the calm surf
watch the crab vanish underwater
beautiful as memory, while every
mother places their hands on their
child's head in protection.

Holy

It is the first summer Sunday
in this new world

I wait in a cone of uncertainty
for a hurricane to birth its wind

against our door, so this morning
before the clouds form, I gather

the ripening tomatoes, the quickening
cucumbers off the vine, because

this is what I've been taught to do
by Virginian mothers. As I fill my arms

cradling the still warm sun, I kneel in this dirt
bow my head to these leaves, pray

to the blowing weeds. Take communion
in this calm

I have grown.

Tropical Depression

Today, on a stepladder in the dirt
I washed windows. The last step
in the cleaning and clearing of a well lived-in
home. The hurricane creeps up the shore,
humidity clings like spiderwebs,
wasps fall with my rags to the ground.

Inside, my mom removes the screens,
works the puzzle of these ancient windows.
We are nose to nose through glass. We
spray and wipe circles in unison. The ashes
in a box. The boxes on a truck. The windows
gleam, we walk away.

Things that have died this month

An American Bullfrog caught in a net in Acris pond, limp in my hands and laid on the shore near a cypress tree. Food for a heron.

At least six turtles. The remnants of their eggs scattered near a shallow hole surrounded by tracks of coyotes and claw marks.

I once read Mary Oliver fried up turtle eggs for breakfast, having dug them from the nest near her favorite pond where she'd watched their mother emerge.

Three rainbow snakes, rotten and decomposing from a disease we try to find the source of. Their faces so disfigured, they'd become unable to feed.

Michael's father in a nursing home where no one could visit him.

A northern water snake with a belly bulge hard from catfish.

The catfish.

The 100-foot pine tree crowded by the canopy of oaks, leaning to the left and dead on the right side. Soon to be ground into woodchips

A fishing spider still clutching a tadpole.

Michael's mother in a nursing home where no one could visit her.

On Mother's Day I wave to my mom at a distance. Slip cucumber sandwiches through her mail slot.

My neighbor, Jean, I talked to only once, handing her a misdirected postcard that I didn't even read.

977 Virginians.

Pollinate

Let me tell you a secret.
Today, I left work early—
(feigned a headache)
so that I could sit
in the garden and watch
the bees tango and tangle
over the unfurling roses
curling in each petal
diving from sweet nectar
dip to sway pollen drunk
and stumbling, butterflies balanced
on zinnias all around I swelled
with sound, all of us, pollinators
what we choose to touch, what is gone
what is found.

Fairytale Rewrite

You think I'm like those girls in forests
lost and haunted leaving
trails of breadcrumbs to be eaten
by the feral unseen. Behind all the trees
you see pointed ears, a curled finger,
the traps and tricks of a troubled mind.

There is no candy house of colored
confections, no campfire ghost
or country outlaw, my woods
are medicine, chapel and haven
congregants of bats and magpies, blankets
of pine I call mine, these trails are sugar

I am the bee. Let me go when I tell you
this is what I need to be found—
Here, berries are currency
squirrels consolers, spiders
spin my hair in silver webs
and I am light again, my heart
open wide. I promise I'll return
to you changed, my freckles
constellations, laugh light
as skipped pebbles, dry-eyed
and smiling I'll reach for you
awake with ever-after sweetness.

Vision

Each time I sit around a campfire, I am hypnotized
into believing I could have survived on my own once

in a cave, creating warmth and light from some sticks
and my skills, some spells I pulled like strands of hair
out of memory—

Then I think of how I can't see without my glasses thick
as limbs, unable to tell a bear from a deer, and surely unable

to see the edge of a cliff from the sky it sits in.

Fig(ure)1

This week I wake early
before the birds, if only
to be first to the ripening
fig tree. Searching the broad leaves
in the slow melting dark. Straining
to see the purple against the sky
how they blur together in this light.
The birds watch from the roof,
the lawn, the wooden house I built
them, waiting for me to leave
the buffet open, two jewels
shining sunlit in my palm.

Thoughts While Standing atop Lover's Leap Trail

—Natural Tunnel, VA

Despite the 3 miles of protective chain link fence, I have
followed on this narrow cliff climb, I still imagine people

scaling it nimbly, perching on the slim rail and jumping
into the yawning cavern below like the legend

the warring tribes, the love that couldn't be in life
what are things that you hear before you see?

The trees shake their arms before you feel the breeze
that moved them, the owls screech like wailing children

as the sun slips behind the carved-out tunnel, leaves click
and curl to cup the coming rain. They are already changing

color, what other ways is dying so beautiful? There is water
flowing somewhere, because I hear it splash makes it so

on the Caution! sign that warns not to throw objects off the cliff
or to lean over, decades of lovers have carved their initials

J + T forever, *no matter what,* and Abbie who has returned
to this very spot four times, etched her name and marked

the date, stopped coming five years ago and I'm so sad
at the missing of her and the low bellowing of the cows

in a meadow that must be on the other side of this void
and the story the Red Stone Diner waitress told me

over my Friday night Fish Fry, that Vivian, who lived
across the railroad tracks jumped from the tunnel

ledge last fall, and no one ever found the whole note she took
with her, it was after her third husband died of the cancer

he was the one, she'd said, loved her better than anyone.

Flash

Tonight, I can't look away
from the flickering star above
my house, which is really a pulsar
the size of New York
whose steady blink
just happens to match
the lone firefly
in the beauty berry bush—
Both of them flash
a Morse code message
to me, swinging beams of light
that remain when my eyes close
wrapped in a sheet of stars.

We are works in progress

After months of quarantine
your hair has gone so long and wavy
it has changed your face and you
malign the feel of it on the back of your neck
how it curls on your pillow when you sleep
pressed against your ears, creeping towards
your cheek, you've taken to wearing
my hair bands to keep the ringlets
from your eyes, and when we ride
our bikes I catch the sparkle
of the silver polka dots on my headband smile.

Most weeks we see no one but each other, the cats
fight, then sleep and so do we, feeding each other
with what we can grow or graze or fish and the longer
your hair grows the wilder we are in our quiet
cocoon. The full moon slants in through our blinds
bathes your head in halo light and I whisper a wish
to each hair, a prayer to each wave and I swear
each morning it grows longer and I am so much stronger
I don't ever need to sleep.

When you are finally allowed to sit in your barber's chair
have him use the number three razor to shear your neck
and sides, he calls you "Curly," as it falls
in rings around the chair. You come home smelling
of powder and limes, crisp as fall, school's first day
I realize now I hardly knew you at all.

Nocturnal Pantoum

It was troublesome how she could hide
vanished then cocooned in silk
a lime robbed of light
letting go feels like forgiveness
vanished then cocooned in silk
our best glow is by moonlight
letting go feels like forgiveness

forgetting feels like taking flight

our best glow is by moonlight
a lime robbed of light
forgetting feels like taking flight
It was troublesome how she could hide

Linger

I have spent the day in one place
watching the shadows of the porch rail
slats shift from right to left
letting the side of my face sunburn
in this treetop perch birdsong
becomes language I feel for
with the tip of my tongue, forgotten
words that tickle my throat like feathers
so that by the time I am back in shadow
I have learned how to fly, how to hunt
how to feed by small mouthfuls
the hungriest needs.

Fig(ure)2

Promise me, we'll never become
accustomed to the figs, never
stop being astonished each August
when they burst to ripe bulbs below
their leaves flagrant in their flesh-
pound and mission, Turkish and Calimyrna.

Each bite, each sticky drip of sap, each time
we reach high to find the day's gift, we'll remember
the first time we kissed this bliss of sun
each one more sweet
more difficult to reach.

How each of us had been picked
by hand as one.

Grow

It has rained so much the grass is wild
carpet thick and tangled with the late summer
confetti of crepe blossoms. If I stay
at this early morning window
gazing long enough
I'm convinced I can see
the grass growing—
each blade waving me out
until I can't resist the pull
feeling my bare feet sink
deep leaving impressions
on the lawn, divots soft as rabbits
pocks of moles tunneling below me.
I press myself down
emboss my skin with August.

Phantom

My mom's amputated finger often hurts
worse is when it itches
or the ring she used to wear
constricts her. She cut it once
on broken glass, and some days
(touching the void as she tells me)
she'll feel the raised skin of that scar
the hangnail she still tries to bite or tear
the cuticle ridge she wishes
to push into a perfect crescent moon.

This is how I know I'll feel what's gone.

Butterfly Rose

Is it wing or petal
antennae or thorn-
what would one be
without the other?

Desperate bee, flock of gulls
and all around the pear falls
apart, the peaches unravel
bud becomes bug becomes
bloom.

I would kneel for you
I would joust for you
somewhere in the vanishing
point, we are one.

If I lift my wing you bear fruit.

All of the animals I have seen this summer come to visit

In the dunes, the coyote ambles in shadow, looks up, sniffs and lopes over the sand. The same day my grandmother died I saw a fox, patient and still at the end of the cul-de-sac watching.

The bobcat was blur and ear tufts and stub tail, it leapt in my path and vanished.

When the rabbits arrived I said come in, come in, slow your beating hearts, your twitching nose and nervous paws, do not startle at the sound of sobbing. Let me make you a plate, all berries and garnish.

I will drink lemongrass tea, you will slurp broth of carrots and celery. I will serve you all of the things I can grow, if you stay. The snakes turn the soil, make it fertile and dark. The tops of the beet fronds, don't ever discard, I'll sauté for the turtles who'll dine by the moon.

The egret will roost in the rafters, the herons will hover and dive, deliver bullfrogs and bluegill each night. Come in, coyote. Why would I run from you? Especially now, when I've been all alone. See my face is bare, the breath you feel, I swear, is clean, and these tears just keep my teapot full. I am happy, I whisper in your fur. Even if my lips tremble it's just my muscle memory forgetting how to smile. I will practice.

Bobcat and Barred Owl unravel all the yarn from my scarves, take my sweaters, stay up all night chasing mice. Have you eaten, Gray Fox? (This is how I greet all visitors now). Come, let me make you a plate of wild garlic and soft-boiled eggs deconstructed, yolk and albumen divided on a plate of bone China with a hand-painted forest scape.

It is a small thing to share a meal. How much more will I know you, when I watch you eat

with pleasure what I've made with my hands. Will you stay? If it means I must carve

my own heart into morsels, lay it in a path like breadcrumbs from your den, I would do it,

again and again.

Trust

I do not have a green thumb
despite my love of plants
they don't thrive in my care
either smothered by my hovering
overwatered, a little
too much love and sun
or forgotten in the dark
each brittle leaf rusted crisp
and collected on the floor-

which is why, when my mother-in-law
gave me the family Christmas cactus
so robust and reaching, ancient and heirloom
she was telling me, even I, could nurture life.

EKG

For two long minutes
twice a day when I brush my teeth
with the electric toothbrush and its perfect
30 second interval pulses for each quadrant of my mouth
I think how it is the exact amount of time that you were dead
arrested on a hospital bed while a 4 foot nothing nurse straddled
you

and pounded your heart back to life. Now your pacemaker keeps
track of each beat

and somewhere in the sky a satellite watches it spike and dip, a
wave we ride, a grave we cheat.

Fig(ure)3

These are instructions for joy:
I would encourage you, if not urge
you to eat a fig plucked
from a summer tree
warmed by August light
washed by moonglow and sweet
bliss relief of drought's last gasp.

Don't think of the wasp
the fig can't live without
entering the small passage
to lay its eggs, or the offspring
tunneling pollen out, broken
winged and spent, think
of the sweet burst as a reverse
blossom, a flower that has bloomed
on your tongue alone

When I die I want to be buried in a mushroom suit

The days of rain stop suddenly
and mushrooms appear overnight
in the toppled trees, in the waterlogged
woods, marshy and ripe with rot
my eyes become sharp and trained
spotting lion's mane and lobster
leaning in to inspect the gills tender
lamella releasing spores like smoke
in the September woods after summer's
last sigh, mushrooms bloom on all that dies
and having spent the summer learning
how to tell a grape vine, from a trumpet,
Virginia Creeper from coral honeysuckle
streaks of greenbrier thorn still raw on my cheek
I want to know these mushrooms like family
like my child I could pick from a crowd anywhere
from the back of her head, the curve of his ear
so I get down on my knees, press my palms

to the mud, scan the ground for morels and black trumpets
breathing in this smell, the duff and pine, the decay
and the life, until it has all soaked through me, my damp
skin, my body so still a wood beetle crawls up my arm
I find the ridges of turkey tail, the crimson of cinnabar
chantarelle and the closer I look, the more green I see
everything teeming. Between life and death, the mushrooms
are crossing guards, as if they had yellow vests, a whistle
and orange waving flags; hello stump, mud snake,
opossum, right this way. I lay my head down

now, I lay me down, not to ash, dust and teeth
grave wax and nylon threads, but on September
soil, hen of the woods, oyster, honey—home.

Some Advice

Dear K,

How have you been sleeping?
My doctor recommended
chamomile or kava before bed.

Each night, I roll, a drunken ship
a blown feather, my ups and downs
of dread. I'm told I'm not alone

in this and I'd like to think of someone
else sitting in the blue dark sipping tea
holding the warmth of a bloomed flower.

Love,

K

Propagate

On my birthday, my friend gave me
a small terracotta pot brimming
with the offspring of her spider plant
each variegated stem dangling delicate
and tender. She hands it to me gently
says, *my plant had babies,* then quickly

looks away, guilty, says she keeps having
déjà vu. I cradle the gift, believe I feel
spiders crawling on my arm. *I will try*

to keep it alive, I say. These plants
don't need much, they can tolerate abuse.

More

Coffee, thank you.
I could sit in a corner
admit almost that in some way
old stories could be proved fact
in the wild. Cream, dipped
spoon, hope. I can hold the joy
dear, of us, kind. Loving in French
speaking in smiles.

Perfection, still

We stand in the garden where my love grew
up knee deep in dirt and native plants
the air full of fritillaries having their own parade
waving bannered wings and conducting a choir
of bees, my mother-in-law raises pollinators
and earthworms, every green and fruiting thing
for them to feed on and dance twirling pollen
from pistil to stamen and all around us common

milkweed, Asclepias, from the Greek god of medicine
seeds split and parachute in wind and we kneel to examine
the underside of each leaf, finding monarch eggs so small
they could pass through the eye of a needle
we thread our lives together and every summer we repeat
this ritual and finally something feels normal, this cycle
is still egg to caterpillar to chrysalis
to wings drying in the sun
we grasp these newly hatched
monarchs like lifting grains of sand
look for the two black spots of the male
which you hold, I check mine, pray they'll mate

little lights beating orange on our wrists
you have three weeks, you have this launch

and loft, you have this time only now of flutter
breath, this night on a jumpy video I hold in my hand

I watch my nephew heart beating, down
on one knee, ask the question
she turns towards him all sun and nectar
still joy, this yes, this delight in future
in tomorrow, in tomorrow

Fig(ure)4

I believe in the abundance of the fig tree
how it gives and gives until we have all
had our fill; the birds are gorged, the squirrels
sticky with sap and purple paws as they wobble
towards a nap in the curtain of these leaves
big as my head, and everything left that I can reach
fat and bursting I pluck for preserves
shining in jars I will dip in all winter long
there is nothing I won't slather it on.

M-I-S-S-I-N-G

I love how my husband's Greek family signs off a call
    with *many kisses,* how in person they give them
        forehead, cheek, sometimes ear lobe pecks

    In Spanish, *besitos* are little kisses, every greeting
comes with a side of smooches. There's French, obviously
not just *that* one, to know the pleasure of a tongue hummed

but the soft press of barely lip to barely cheek
    air kisses we blow, catch dramatic and clutch
        to the heart with a cloud of sighs, like perfume

        that exhales like breath when in kissing distance
now my eyes sigh, water my cheeks pink, behind
my mask, my lips dry out, lipstick crumbles to powder

My mom has always blotted her lipstick
    on anything around, all my life I've found
        her lip prints on scraps of paper; envelopes, the power bill

        countless grocery receipts, the checkbook ledger
how she'd press the paper or tissue to her mouth
splotch the ridged impression of her lips, I swear I'd know
anywhere

and even now in the glove box of my car
    I find my registration with the faint pink outline of her kiss
        I miss it. Resuscitate: 15 compressions and two breaths

    We sign off our messages with x's, *many kisses*
we save these x's in text, a treasure map marked
a blown wish on a lone candle on a cut cake, we still celebrate

In the end

We are miscellaneous
clutter
some spoons
almost new underwear
a quilt with a wagon-wheel pattern
a box of pictures

regret
and papers still waiting for attention.

Equinox

On the day both halves of this planet receive the sun's rays equally
Persephone returns to her husband in the underworld.

Above light is stretching its long fingers into every darkness
in strict measure lighting corner cobwebs, sparking deserts golden

rivers dazzle blaze and mountains gleam gauzy in light. Each
window in this world, an equal day an equal night, but some rank

more equal than others, hasn't that always been the way? That little
bit of lingering light a minute here, three minutes there, a trick a
swindle, a deal with the devil lips bright with pomegranate. At dawn
rise from a vigil

the wisps of a dying fire brought in on hair, the cool night and smoke
on skin

eyes will be stars, crawl into bed, ankles bound with vines, a trail of
petals turned

to ash, make darkness honey sweet, do all you can to please, just
don't lie and say its equal.

This is just a reminder

that as the leaves fall, be
still, let them be homes for
bees who haven't actually gone
anywhere but spend the winter in nests
their mothers made, essential for shelter
for bumble bee queens, butterflies and moths.
Leave the leaves for lady beetles to live perfectly
placed to attack aphids when your spring garden
grows. Leave the logs and wood piles, the knotty
bumps are abode to dozens of praying mantis
whose hunger you'll want come summer
and just in case the legend is true
they are signs of an angel come
to visit you, or the compass to
point a lost child home, leave
them, simply tell guests
excuse my mess, I'm
creating habitats.

The Farmer's Almanac Predicts a Cold Winter

So do my apples with their tough skins and the sweet
corn with its thick husk, all the collected nuts
from summer squirrels, a Carolina Wren who returns
each year to nest in the corners of my porch
right now, September is second summer, Hell's back
deck and shaking hands is over, so is the elbow bump
a 90-degree angle that catches our sneeze and cradles
our cough. I narrowly dodge a bear hug from a friend
I hadn't seen in months, so warm was his smile and arms
outstretched I almost forgot to duck and weave away
I so missed his barrel chest, his grandfather scruff
and aftershave. I no longer fall asleep to the Norfolk-Southern

trains or wake to airport noise. It's easier now to hear birds
and cicadas shaking loose from their shells. I wonder if I could
build a bunk bed in the shed, make it a Tiny Home all shabby chic
and lose an hour following a trail of ants to the remnants of a cherry
sucker still packaged and dissolved from the heat.

I once kept a giant ring pop on my nightstand, licked it sticky every
morning. Goodnight Moon I'll love you forever, Rainbow Fish. I am
paralyzed by the thought of calling my mom only to realize she has
died. I walk to the edge of a cliff, to the rail

of a bridge and hear myself whispering me over. This city's
mermaids sparkle, splash, don flowers, and parade on every postcard
and mural. In the park I find a ripped tent, a cat, an open book of
hymns. In a closet full of dresses I never wear, I rustle the ruffles
and tulle to hear them swish and straps spaghetti-thin slide from
hangers, I abandon them for uniforms and paper masks.

I spend too much time wishing Alex Trebek is not dead and I'm
angry that the heat index is 106 and the leaves are not falling

and above me the arc of geese are returning home and I believe there will be snow this winter.

Newborn

These days I celebrate
each living thing
the soft tuft of rabbit
I see at dusk peeking
from under the shed.
The restless nestlings
hatching in the bird house
by the bedroom window
that wake me each day
in hunger. We don't need
storks and bonnets, parades
or applause to start again
minute by minute, a newborn
full of wonder.

Waiting for a turkey to defrost

Ponder moderation while eating cereal from the gravy boat.

Consider rewritten histories. Make a list of gratitude:

The symmetry of buttonholes, street sweepers, sleep.

Press it to your palm. Trace your hand with markers
on Chinese take-out menus.

Make a garland of paper turkeys. Pardon them all for your crimes.

Make a crown of napkin feathers. Give your turkey a bath. Chip the
ice with a ladle, a pie server, decorative corn cob holders.

Remember you are eating alone. Take a walk, instead take a drive.

Keep driving. Find a field or farm. Eat acorns, chestnuts,
sweet grass. Lie on the ground, listen to the wind. Count
the birds flying overhead, name them alphabetically
until you fall asleep, finally thawed.

A cure for blue

I have taken to filling the house
with flowers, so that every room
has some life. In the golden light
of sunrise, I will walk east to west
through my shoebox house and watch
as petals turn to watercolors casting prisms
shifting red to yellow
orange to salmon
on the old grain of these floors
so for one moment of each day
I can step a bare toe into that light
and bathe in joy.

Lessons

December 2020

I am a substitute in this last week of school before winter break.
It is fancy dress day and my body sparkles in sequins with tulle
on my hips and shoes clicking bright down the hallway.
I roll this borrowed art cart into kindergarten classes.
I smile with my eyes, shout through thick cotton
and filters to 16 children in princess dresses

and tuxedos, old-man suspenders and shining tiaras.
We play dress up to wish away a year without hugs

and hidden smiles. Their desks: little clear cages of plexiglass.
Their eyes peer up at me for the lesson I've been left

by their teacher: artist and caregiver, now patient alone.
I am here telling them to draw an oval in the corner.

An oval is an egg, is an eye, is an avocado.
We draw a larger oval around the first,

which is now a bagel, a sushi roll, Saturn.
Draw a line out from the top of the oval

straight and true, mirror the oval's curve
on the other side. We see a cylinder, a soda

can, a hot dog bun. We draw a wavy line
down the center of the page: an unfurling roll

a magic carpet unwound, a flag in the wind.
Match the wavy line on the other side, connect

the ends, wait as they laugh, recognize the familiar
toilet paper unrolled and waving goodbye to this year.

Goodbye to missing and distance, goodbye to fear—these
paper squares as symbols, our landscape paper as witness.

This is what artists do, capture this moment now,
as we pretend in our year's best clothes

our covered face, our careful space. A mask is armor
is kindness, is costume. A belief that a cape will make

us fly. Let's pretend! We dance and twirl, we substitute,
we draw all the things we have missed, lost, wish.

This week we are hope. We are small circles of light
dancing off sequins shining into new.

Humbled

I have just learned and wanted
to share, that if you are feeling
melancholy, you can now see
what the Hubble telescope
held for a second in its lens
on your birthday, and it is as magnificent
as you might imagine, a collision
between two spiral galaxies
that began 700 million years ago
caught in all its scatter light, aqua gold shimmer
a crash of a candle on a pillow of frosting
wished out, from your breath, you small thing.

Colloquial

In the gray January gloaming, I walk the seven blocks to the post office carrying my boxes awkwardly. The pink sneakers I've swapped my office heels for, kiss the concrete and the people I pass smile so bright behind their masks, I see their eyes light. My legs are all marigold sun winking with my pink-shoed stride. People wave like our hands were drawn up by invisible strings, by magnets pulling us together. *I like your stockings, baby,* they say. The old woman and the man on the stoop, have I ever said *stockings?* A word my grandma used, she was never without stockings well into her 90s, her sensible pumps and her four-foot-nothing frame, stockings in summer swelter or Pennsylvania blizzard, snowdrifts of stockings. On this old street, cracked cobblestones and closed up shops, the texture of a city dusty and worn, the people jangled, but fighting, friendly the ones who can't stop grinning at my daffodil tights, mid-winter sigh—the people I pass, nod, wave, say, *I like them stockings,* they leave me smiling all day as I veil them under my desk, legs glowing bright, warm.

Meadow

This March when our ground was still cold
and sleeping I learned how to drive a tractor
plow a field and till the soil up in rows
a giant needle sewing in backstitch
which is not so different from sowing me.
From my palms I tossed the seeds for native plants
the mountain mint and milkweed, yarrow and aster.
Tiny black specks lost to the dirt, everything fallow.

After months of shut-in, how astonished I was
to find a meadow burst from earth
trembling with wings.

About the Author

Kindra McDonald is the author of the books *Fossils* and *In the Meat Years* (both published in 2019) and the chapbooks *Elements and Briars* (2016) and *Concealed Weapons* (2015). She received her MFA from Queens University of Charlotte. She is an Adjunct Professor of Writing and teaches poetry at The Muse Writers Center in Norfolk, VA. She served as Regional VP of the Virginia Poetry Society and was the recipient of the 2020 Haunted Waters Press Poetry Award. She lives in the city of mermaids with her husband and cats where she bakes, hikes, and changes hobbies monthly.

You can find her in the woods or at www.kindramcdonald.com.